A FUNNY THING HAPPENED ON THE WAY TO COMMUNION

Finding Subtle Humor in the Bible

Dale T. Stanton

ISBN 978-1-63885-527-9 (Paperback)
ISBN 978-1-63885-528-6 (Digital)

Covenant Books, Inc.
11661 Hwy 707
Murrells Inlet, SC 29576
www.covenantbooks.com

It is the glory of God to conceal things…

—Proverbs 25:2a (NRSV)

CONTENTS

INTRODUCTION

Ever laugh in church? Perhaps it was a little snickering when a child says something funny during the children's sermon or when the pastor gives a humorous illustration in his sermon. However, did you ever laugh when the Bible itself was being read?

The Old Testament lesson was 1 Samuel 3:1–10, the account of the Lord appearing to the young Samuel. As the pastor read verse 8, "…and the Lord called Samuel again," someone's mobile phone rang. The timing couldn't have been more precise. I'm sure I heard a few snickers.

We probably don't think of the Holy Bible as a book to make people laugh, nor remotely funny. Quite the opposite, from beginning to end, we see the stamp of human sinfulness and its consequential evil throughout the history of mankind.

It's amazing that in this book we call *holy*, we find such unholy behavior: stories of rebellion, murder, wars, greed, lust, demon possession, adultery, conniving, cowardice, and every other kind of human depravity, reaching its apex in the suffering and crucifixion of God's beloved Son, Jesus the Christ.

However, the Bible declares Jesus's crucifixion and resurrection as the ultimate victory over sin, death, and the power of the devil. It is the watershed event of all human history—past, present, and future.

Sadly, many people miss that last point. How could a loving God allow so much evil and suffering in the world? They view the Bible as a mere collection of myths and fairy tales reflecting the pathetic debased condition of humankind. Nevertheless, the Bible affirms there is a divine plan running through its pages—that the hand of God is at work to redeem the world for Himself. There is a

German term for it: *Heilsgeschichte* or holy history—the history of our salvation.

On the evening of His resurrection, Jesus encountered two disciples on the road to Emmaus, as recorded in Luke 24. While walking, Jesus opened their minds to the Scriptures, explaining that everything written up to that moment pointed toward Him. Verse 27 states, "And beginning at Moses and all the prophets, He expounded to them in all the Scriptures the things concerning Himself." Later, in writing his gospel, John declares, "these things were written that you may believe that Jesus is the Christ, the Son of God, and that believing you may have life in His name."

Indeed, the Bible is the record of God working through ordinary human beings like you and me to carry out His divine plan of salvation. It never ceases to amaze me how God not only works through us, but in spite of us to accomplish His will and purposes, considering our sinfulness and lack of faith.

This humanness of the characters in the Bible particularly intrigues me, as we discover their inner doubts, fears, and struggles and especially their faithlessness. I think to myself, *These people are just like me.* I see myself reflected in them. At times, the things the biblical characters say and do are downright funny, though quite unintentional, I'm sure.

I began to notice this comical slant in the personalities of the Bible after sitting in church so many years hearing the Scripture lessons read. Many of those times were spent while I was sitting on an organ bench. You see, I am a church organist, having played the organ in church even before I could drive. I became keenly aware of the subtle humor in the Bible, when, as the lessons were being read by the pastor or the lector, I spontaneously almost burst out laughing, as if someone had just told a funny joke. At times I literally put my hand over my mouth to stifle an audible laughter. I would think to myself, *Oh my gosh, that is hilariously funny!* Yet it seemed to me I was the only one who caught it. The rest of the congregation sat in stone-faced silence while I sat there chuckling to myself.

Maybe it's because people think that to laugh in church just isn't right, especially as the Bible is being read. Wouldn't that be sacrilegious or disrespectful? I guess because most people just don't expect the Bible to be amusing, and therefore, do not discern the subtle snippets of wit and humor imbedded in its discourse that suddenly jumps out at you, or at least, me. Oftentimes I will come home from church and share with my wife Beth some newly discovered humor I heard in a particular scripture lesson read that morning. She will usually respond with a quizzical look that means, "Okay, if you say so."

In Proverbs 25:2, wise King Solomon declared that "it is the glory of God to conceal things." He seems to suggest there are great and glorious nuggets of truth which God takes delight in *hiding* from us. By His grace, He has given us an inquiring mind to explore, investigate, and seek out these hidden gems in order for us to discover more about Him and learn from His word.

I have decided that these indirect and elusive treasures of biblical humor read in church need to be shared with the general populace, and thus, the purpose for writing this book. Whether or not you share my brand of humor doesn't matter (although that would be quite complimentary). What does matter is that through the stories and the accounts I have shared in the book, you may develop a keener awareness of and a deeper appreciation for our God who works through all kinds of avenues—even humor—in working out yours and my salvation.

I have striven to not come across as preachy and sanctimonious. I tried to avoid imperative language. After all, who am I but a fellow traveler on the Christian life road, "pressing on toward the goal for the prize of the heavenly call of God in Christ Jesus?" (Philippians 3:4 NRSV). With the apostle Paul, I view myself as the "foremost of sinners" (1 Timothy 1:15). If at times I sound protreptic, I am speaking to myself as well and from my own flawed life experience. Most often, I quote from the Scripture to supersede my own finite wisdom. I've attempted to inject some humor of my own to lighten things up (which I hope you may find amusing). I even composed a limerick to summarize each chapter. I've titled this book *A Funny Thing Happened on the Way to Communion*. I can't take credit for it. It was devised by my smart and witty son, Benjamin.

In ancient Israel, worship was meant to be joyful. After God led the children through the Red Sea, Miriam, Aaron's sister, pulls out her tambourine and instantly composes a song of victory (Exodus 15:20–21) with exuberant singing and dancing.

As I scan through the Psalms, it's apparent worship was very vivacious, with much physical movement. In Psalm 126:2, we read, "Then our mouth was filled with laughter, and our tongue with shouts of joy." It's known as a Song of Ascents. The people are celebrating their joyful return to Jerusalem from their Babylonian exile. They are laughing and singing with great jubilation.

It's pretty clear no one was afraid to laugh in worship back then. Now maybe, some Sunday I'll hear someone else giggling (dare I use the word *laughing*?) in church, along with me, chuckling from the organ bench.

Dale Stanton

Addendum: The Scripture readings referenced herein are based on the Revised Common Lectionary, a three-year cycle of weekly lections used to varying degrees by the vast majority of mainline Protestant churches in Canada and the United States.

The What Party?

So, when Peter went up to Jerusalem, the
circumcision party criticized him.

—Acts 11:2 (ESV)

Now this one really made me laugh. The circumcision party? C'mon. Get real. We're used to the Democratic party, the Republican party, the Libertarian party, the Independent party, the Green party, but the circumcision party? What in the world was that?

Apparently in the early church, there was the hot debate over whether or not non-Jews, the gentiles, first had to circumcise in order to become Christians (at least the male population, that is). Of course, back then women had no status whatsoever, so they didn't even enter the picture. At least they had the advantage of avoiding this little surgical procedure.

The diehards weren't about to budge on the matter and took Peter to task for letting these outsiders into the church and corrupt everything. Peter responded by telling them of a dream he had wherein he could kill and eat any kind of food he wanted; it didn't have to be kosher. Essentially, he argued the old Jewish laws no longer applied to the gentiles, that the Gospel is a gift to all people—Jew and gentile alike.

There may not be any circumcision parties in the church today, but it is not uncommon to find cliques, in-groups, and inner circles in which some folks are made to feel welcome and others are excluded, either intentionally or inadvertently. My family and I were members of a congregation for several years wherein I also served as organist and director of music. During the whole time, we often felt like we were on the outside looking in. Not a good thing.

The church is and always should be the one place, the one group, the one family on earth where anyone and everyone is not only welcomed, but included and valued. Sure there are different organizations, groups, and committees that function within the congregation and that members can hook up with depending on individual needs and interests. But in the final analysis, every member must share in the same high status of being part of the family of God, no matter what. As the old adage goes, "Family is the place you are always welcome."

For a little sideline amusement, in the Lutheran church body of which I am a part, January 1—New Year's Day—is designated as Circumcision and Name of Jesus, based upon Luke 2:21 (NRSV), "After eight days had passed, it was time to circumcise the child; and he was called Jesus, the name given by the angel before he was conceived in the womb."

In most church denominations who follow the Revised Common Lectionary, the word *circumcision* is left out and the festival is simply noted as Name of Jesus.

I certainly can understand how keeping the word *circumcision* in the title could leave some folks a little uncomfortable. In your New Year's celebrations, I suppose if you greeted someone with "Happy Circumcision Day," they might think you're crazy. Also, I've never seen a Hallmark greeting card commemorating the event. It would be a challenge creating the message on the inside.

There once was a party called circumcision
In church, it caused some division.
But Peter concluded, no one is excluded
From receiving the Great commission.

BLESSED ARE THE WHO?

When Jesus saw the crowds, he went up the mountain;
and after he sat down, his disciples came to him. Then
he began to speak, and taught them, saying...
—Matthew 5:1–11NRSV

Matthew 5 contains the famous Sermon on the Mount. Another version is found in Luke 6:20–23. Known as The Beatitudes, verses 1–11 of Matthew's account begin with the word *blessed*. A few English translations substitute the word *happy* for *blessed*. So who are the blessed or the happy ones?

Actually, there's nothing in this account that I find laughable. However, I find it ironic (irony is a kind of wry amusement) how many Christians equate material wealth with blessings from God. Glorying in their accumulation of worldly goods and of their own achievements, they boast, "We are so blessed." Really?

Who did *Jesus* say are the blessed? Somehow I don't think Jesus was referring to those living in their pretentious dream home, not the ones with the overpriced posh vehicle in the driveway, not those who take luxurious vacations every year, or who have climbed the social ladder to live it up with their six-figure incomes. Does that mean all these "blessings" really are not signs that God has rewarded us?

Back to the Sermon on the Mount, Jesus redresses all false illusions of what it means to be truly blessed. Blessed are the ones who are broken and who seek God. Blessed are the sad who have experienced loss so that God can fill their loss with Himself. Blessed are those who are kind and merciful, who strive to do the right thing. Blessed are those who are content with what they have and don't covet for more. Blessed are those whose hearts are pure and consciences clean. Blessed are those who work for peace and harmony. Blessed are those who suffer scorn and rejection for following God's ways—they will ultimately be rewarded. All this certainly is a far cry from the common and assumed belief of what it means to be blessed.

In another place, Jesus offers us further enlightenment on the matter. In Mark 10, Jesus had a conversation with a man who thought he had it made in the shade. Jesus said he was missing the most important thing of all, which could only be gained by giving all his possessions to the poor and following Jesus. In that way, Jesus said, he will have true heavenly wealth. (You can also read about it in Matthew 19 and Luke 18—the story of the rich young man.)

Are you blessed? Am I blessed? It all depends on whether our concept of being blessed is in accordance with Jesus. What *is* true blessedness? Who else than Jesus should we go to for the correct answer?

Jesus had just finished driving out a demon. He then teaches how an evil spirit can leave a person but return with seven more spirits accompanying him, leaving the person worse off than the beginning. Hearing this, a woman in the crowd cries, "How happy is the woman who bore you and nursed you!"

Jesus responds by saying, "Rather, how happy (blessed) are those who hear the word of God and obey it!" (Luke 11:27–28 GNT).

These words of Jesus are paraphrased so well in the hymn "How Blest Are They Who Hear God's Word," penned by Johan Nordahl Brun (1745–1816).

> "How blest are they who hear God's Word,
> Who keep in faith what they have heard,
> Who daily grow in wisdom.
> From light to light they shall increase
> And journey on life's way in peace;
> They have the oil of gladness
> To soothe their pain and sadness."

Looking for real blessedness and true happiness? Listen to God's Word and follow it!

The Beatitudes Jesus spoke
To those who were common folk
Those whom in Jesus would rest
Are they who are truly blest.
'Tis better to wear Jesus' yoke.

Timing Is Everything

> At that time Emperor Augustus ordered a census to be
> taken throughout the Roman Empire. When this first
> census took place, Quirinius was the governor of Syria.
> —Luke 2:1–2 (NIV)

"Get me to the church on time." Remember that song from the 1956 musical *My Fair Lady*? It was sung by Alfred P. Doolittle. The song is a plea to his friends to make sure he gets to the church for his wedding.

So you have to get there no matter what. It may be a wedding, a funeral (preferably a wedding), a doctor's appointment, a job interview, whatever. It may be a long trip. Timing is of the essence. You can't let weather, car trouble, traffic, or flight delays stop you. I wonder if this is how God felt while preparing for His Son's entry into the world?

After hearing the Christmas story countless times, nothing about it struck me as being funny at all. Quite the contrary, it is a very serious account fraught with drama and even danger. Everything in the story had to come together at the right time to fulfill all the ancient prophecies.

The timing had to be precise. "When the right time came, the time God decided on," we read in Galatians 4:4 (TLB). The place was not open for discussion. It had to be Bethlehem. "O Bethlehem Ephrathah, you are but a small Judean village, yet you will be the birthplace of my King who is alive from everlasting ages past!" (Micah 5:2 TLB).

The trouble is, Mary and Joseph were not in Bethlehem, but living in Nazareth, about seventy miles north. How was God going to get them from Nazareth to Bethlehem at just the right time? Well, how about a census? And so, the plan unfolded.

For no earthly reason, the Roman emperor, Caesar Augustus, decreed that a census must be taken throughout the empire. Quirinius was governor of the province of Syria (not sure why he's mentioned, but Luke was a stickler on details). By law, Joseph had to return to his hometown to be registered in the census. And where was that? Bethlehem! Despite Mary's advanced pregnancy, the two had to get to Bethlehem no matter what, and to get there posthaste. Probably Mary and Joseph thought they were going to Bethlehem simply to obey the law, not cognizant of the larger picture of fulfilling God's holy plan.

The mind-blowing miraculous thing about this whole story— and this is where the humor comes in—is how God used this cold-hearted, pagan king of the known world to orchestrate a plan, which affected every citizen of the empire—the entire inhabited earth—to get Mary and Joseph to Bethlehem so that Jesus would be born where the prophets said he would be born. Now that's funny, not in the comical, rolling-on-the-floor-laughing sense, but in the kind of way that puts a grin on your face and makes you think, *Now isn't that just the most amazing thing?*

For the skeptics who think this whole thing was just some colossal coincidence or accident or that God isn't involved in the affairs of the world or that he doesn't use the world powers that be to accomplish His will, take a look at the Christmas story! Everything was planned and carried out to the precise detail at the precise time. He truly does have the whole world in His hands.

As a footnote, we know that after Jesus was born, Mary and Joseph and the child returned to Nazareth where Jesus was raised. That, too, was no accident, but part of God's overall plan. "And he (Joseph) went and lived in a town called Nazareth. So was fulfilled what was said through the prophets, that He (Jesus) would be called a Nazarene" (Matthew 2:23 NIV).

According to Nan Corbitt Allen, "Most scholars agree that there are more than three hundred Old Testament prophecies that predicted the coming of the Messiah. When you read them and then compare those to events recorded in the New Testament that are obvious fulfillments of the prophecies, it's truly amazing to see God's plan revealed!"

Some years ago, *Reader's Digest* ran a story about the artwork some very young children drew depicting the Christmas story. One child made a drawing of a big airplane in which through the window, you could see the Holy Family. The Sunday school teacher inquired about the reason for the airplane. The child replied that the airplane depicted the family's *flight into Egypt* to escape the wrath of King Herod (Matthew 2:13–14).

"And who is the man sitting in the front of the plane?" asked the teacher. Somewhat indignantly, the boy responded, "Everyone knows that is PONTIUS, the PILOT!"

> The couple was great with child
> The Son of God undefiled
> To Bethlehem to be enrolled,
> They went as Scripture had foretold
> Prophecy and event reconciled.

No El Cheapo Wine Served Here

> Everyone serves the best wine first. When people are drunk, the host serves cheap wine. But you have saved the best wine for now.
> —John 2:10 (GW)

I always get a kick out of this parable every time it's read: Jesus turning water into wine at the wedding in Cana. John is the only one who reports it. I wonder why? The part I like best is when the master of ceremonies exclaims to the bridegroom about the newly served wine: "Wow, this is really fantastic! Usually the best wine is served first. After everyone is buzzed and can't tell the difference anymore, they drag out the cheap stuff. But you're different. You've saved the best wine until now!" (my paraphrase).

Whether or not that actually was the practice back then—serving the best wine first, then the bottom-of-the-shelf stuff—or whether the host was just trying to be funny, we really don't know. The fact is, the wine Jesus made was top-of-the-line, equivalent to a superlative cabernet sauvignon. (I had to look that up; I really don't know anything about wine.) Of course that shouldn't be surprising. God does not make junk. He doesn't look for the cheapest way or the easiest way, especially when it comes to the redemption of humankind. Only the very best will do. That's why He sent His Son, Jesus, not only to save us from sin, death, and the power of the devil, but to give abundant and everlasting life as well.

The Christian writer, Charles M. Sell, said it so well in his book, *Unfinished Business* (1989). Sell wrote:

> If our greatest need had been information, God
> would have sent an educator. If our greatest need

had been technology, God would have sent us a scientist. If our greatest need had been money, God would have sent us an economist. If our greatest need had been pleasure, God would have sent an entertainer. But since our greatest need was forgiveness, God sent us a Savior.

I remember some years ago when comedian and talk show host Johnny Carson interviewed an eight-year-old boy who was a Christian. The boy exclaimed that he went to Sunday school. Carson asked him, "What are you learning in Sunday school?"

The boy responded, "Last week our lesson was about when Jesus went to a wedding and turned water into wine."

Then Carson asked, "So what did you learn from that lesson?"

The boy paused, smiled, and replied, "If you're going to have a wedding, make sure you invite Jesus!"

From water Jesus made wine,
His first miraculous sign.
This act of sacred story,
Reveals His sublime glory.
Both now and beyond all time.

Going to the Dogs

> He replied, "It is not right to take the children's
> bread and toss it to the dogs."
> "Yes, it is, Lord," she said. "Even the dogs eat the
> crumbs that fall from their master's table."
> —Matthew 15:26–27 (NIV)

I suppose most people would not find this account very humorous. After all, didn't Jesus just call this poor woman a dog? What's so funny about that? I included this passage because it may be one of the most misunderstood passages of the Scripture. A Canaanite woman pleads with Jesus to heal her demon-possessed daughter. Note that because she was a Canaanite, she was regarded by the Jews as a foreigner, an outsider—at the bottom of the totem pole. The disciples urged Jesus to quickly grant her request to shut her up and get her out of the way. Does Jesus do that? No. He refuses, saying that He's too busy to engage taking care of the wayward people of Israel, let alone any foreigners. The desperate woman persists, but Jesus retorts, "It's not right to take the bread away from the children and throw it to the dogs."

Although it may seem so, Jesus was not being disrespectful and insultingly calling this woman a dog. In Greek, the word for *dog* is a diminutive, suggesting a small dog or a puppy. Back then, as today, people had pet dogs or puppies in the house which were fed with scraps of food from the table, much like the way a child today might sneak a piece of food under the table and give it to the pet, unbeknownst to his parents. Jesus is simply saying if you have a choice between feeding your children or the dog, who are you going to feed first? It's a no-brainer: the kids, of course!

But the woman is quick on the draw. "Yes, Lord, but even the dogs are allowed to eat the crumbs that fall."

Response: Jesus marvels at her faith and persistence—maybe even her wit also—and instantly heals her daughter. Persistence.

In many places in the Scripture, Jesus encourages us to pray with persistence, not that we can wheedle or manipulate God into giving everything we want, but simply because He cares for us as a loving Father. In Matthew 7:11, Jesus says, "If you who are an imperfect human being know how to give good things to your children, think how much more God wants to give good things to you and all his children!" He always wants that which results in our ultimate good.

There once was a Canaanite mother
Whose faith was like none other.
Her daughter had died;
Jesus made her alive.
Mom's joy, no one could smother.

Jesus, a Debauchee?

The Son of Man came eating and drinking and you say, "Here
is a glutton and a drunkard, a friend of tax collectors and
sinners." But wisdom is proved right by all her children.
—Luke 7:34–35 (NIV)

A website I visited lists 102 names and titles in the Bible given spe-
cifically to Jesus. However, the titles of glutton and drunkard are not
among them. Nevertheless, in Matthew and Luke, Jesus's critics call
him drunkard, glutton, and a friend of tax collectors and sinners
(outcasts). I couldn't help but snicker when I heard this passage read.
I mean, really! Calling Jesus a lush? A boozer? A schmuck who hangs
out with the riffraff? Did they have any idea who they were insulting?
I don't think so.

It seems Jesus just can't win for losing. In spite of all the good
He does or tries to do, the faultfinders keep nitpicking, in search
of ways to discredit Him. Well, don't we all have days in which we
feel the same way, like we just can't win for losing, when even our
best intentions and best efforts are misunderstood or criticized? With
Jesus, you stand in good company.

So how did Jesus handle his antagonists, the scoffers, the nay-
sayers, and the nitpickers? The reaction he conveyed seemed to be,
"Que sera sera." (Now can't you just hear Doris Day singing that?)
Sometimes you're darned if you do and darned if you don't. What
others think or say about you doesn't count for anything. Don't be
swayed by the inconsistencies of negative people. No one can please
them, not even the Son of God! Literally, the passage reads, "Wisdom
is proved right by all her children." God's wisdom is revealed to be
true by its results.

In a movie, a Native American man is giving wise counsel to his young friend. The man tells him, "You worry too much. Don't sweat the small stuff. *Everything* is small stuff."

In other words, do what you believe to be the right thing and let the chips fall where they may. Don't sweat the small stuff. If you're following God's ways, you have nothing to worry about. Truth has a way of winning out and you'll walk away standing tall.

The elite made a point to be blunt,
Of Jesus, they called him a drunk
He consorted with low-life
To give them the true life;
And His words they could not debunk!

Amazing Lack of Faith

He was amazed at their lack of faith.
—Mark 6:6 (NIV)

Now that's a switch. We usually marvel at someone's *great* faith, their unwavering belief, their rock-solid conviction, their unshakeable trust in God. Even Jesus on many occasions praised a person for their great faith. In Matthew 8, a Roman centurion pleaded with Jesus to heal his servant boy. The centurion was confident that Jesus could heal him without even coming to his home simply by giving the healing command. Jesus was amazed at that, and exclaimed that He had not found such great faith even in Israel. That must have dealt a blow to the listening crowd that a pagan Roman army officer had more faith than that of God's chosen people!

But now we see something different. Jesus had returned to his hometown of Nazareth where he is rejected by his family and friends (Mark 6:1–4). Apparently, Jesus attempted to perform some miracles but couldn't do so because of their unbelief. (However, Mark records He did heal a few people, nevertheless.) Jesus is astonished at their unbelief and lack of faith.

I can't help thinking that at times, Jesus is astonished at my lack of faith as well, maybe even yours? In creation, in His Word and sacraments, He has given us overwhelming evidence of His deep love and care for us. He promises never to leave or forsake us. The cross and empty tomb are the ultimate proof of His love that will not let us go. Yet still, we doubt Him, question Him, invalidate Him, minimize Him, ignore Him, walk away from Him, and don't have time for Him. Or we just go about our daily activity as if our Christian faith has no connection with or bearing on everyday life. To all of us, I think at times Jesus would ask, "Where is your faith?"

A Christian physician observed that next to pain and depression, the most common complaint he heard from his patients was "I can't sleep."

> Jesus and the disciples were on a boat crossing the lake to the other side. An unexpected storm rose up. The boat was being tossed about out of control. The disciples were terrified. But Jesus, apparently exhausted, was sound asleep. The disciples, fearing for their lives, cried out, "Master save us; we are about to die!"
>
> Jesus woke up, commanded the storm to cease, and immediately everything was calm and quiet. Then Jesus asked them, "Where is your faith?" (Luke 8:22–25; paraphrased)

Ouch! I can only imagine the sheepish looks they all must have had.

"He was amazed at their lack of faith," Mark wrote. Hmmm… what would Jesus say about our faith or the lack of it?

> The crowd showed a great deal of skepticism,
> They viewed Jesus with great cynicism.
> To heal and give them relief
> He was amazed at their unbelief.
> And the people remained in their pessimism.

Jesus, the Laughingstock

> He (Jesus) said, "Go away; for the girl is not dead
> but sleeping." And they laughed at him.
> —Matthew 9:24 (NRSV)

Ever laughed at God? In the Bible, it doesn't seem to be too unusual. Abraham and his wife, Sarah, both laughed when told she would bear a son in her old age (Genesis 17:17, 18:12). On the other hand, God also laughs. "The Lord laughs at the wicked, for he knows their day is coming" (Psalm 37:13). Isn't that something? Comedian Woody Allen said, "If you want to make God laugh, tell him your plans." God laughs.

A rabbi of the local synagogue came to Jesus, asking Jesus to bring his dead daughter back to life. Wow! Talk about having faith! By the time Jesus got to the home, the funeral already was underway. When Jesus declared the girl to be only sleeping, the onlookers laughed at him. Other translations say they ridiculed and made fun of him. I can just imagine the guffaws of laughter. Now before passing judgment, wouldn't you and I have done the same? Suppose you were standing by a casket and someone said, "She's not dead, only sleeping?" You probably would have enough respect not to burst out laughing, but you also would probably think, *What, is this guy nuts?*

I'm reminded of a story in which a husband and wife were attending a funeral service. At the conclusion of the service, the pastor announced, "The family will now pass around the bier."

Thinking the pastor was referring to *beer,* the husband whispered to his wife, "I thought they served the beer at the reception!"

God often seems to be the brunt of jokes and derision. Good thing he has broad shoulders. While hanging on the cross, bystanders jeered and made fun of Jesus. Even the bandits who had been crucified with him insulted him (Matthew 27:44). However, in Luke's account, we learn that one of the criminals repented and asked Jesus to remember him when Jesus came into his kingdom (Luke 23:42). Funny how Luke is the only one who mentioned that.

The apostle Paul said the Gospel is regarded as silly nonsense to the unbelieving world. Some deem it as another form of mythology, a fairy tale, certainly nothing to be taken seriously. Christian believers are often regarded as gullible fools.

But God in His wondrous way turns the tables and uses the Gospel to expose and undermine the finiteness and inadequacy of human intelligence and wisdom. It is the seeming absurdity of the cross that in reality is the way of salvation and the ultimate life. (You can read it for yourself in 1 Corinthians 1:21–28.) Now that's nothing to laugh at.

> The dead girl, said Jesus, is sleeping
> The onlookers were quite unbelieving
> They jeered and cracked up until she sat up
> The miracle indeed left them reeling.

ALL THEY CAN DO IS KILL YOU

> I tell you, my friends, do not be afraid of those who kill the
> body but cannot afterward do anything worse. I will show you
> whom to fear: fear God, who, after killing, has the authority
> to throw into hell. Believe me, he is the one you must fear!
> —Luke 12:4–5 (GNT)

I was about thirteen years old sitting in confirmation class when Pastor Range was explaining this passage from Luke. What I remember most is him saying, "Don't be afraid of someone killing you, all they can do is kill you." With that, my friend Dwight and I burst out laughing. Why did we laugh? To a thirteen-year-old, that statement sounds like an absurdity. What possibly could be worse than death? Or someone killing you?

Actually, there is something worse than being murdered or the cessation of the physical body, and that is total separation from God—eternal damnation to put it bluntly. While we may fear any person or force that may cause physical harm, such has no power over our eternal destiny. The one to fear is Jesus, the righteous judge who is our only hope of salvation.

In another place, Philippians 2:12, Paul writes, "Work out your salvation with fear and trembling." He's not suggesting we can earn our salvation—it is always and solely a gift, nothing we can achieve by ourselves (Ephesians 2:8). I think Paul is trying to say we should take our salvation seriously and with deep respect for God, to guard and nourish our spiritual lives as much as we do our physical bodies, to live our lives in Christ with energy and determination, always mindful that one day we will have to give an accounting as we stand

29

before His throne in heaven. "For we will all stand before God's judgment seat" (Romans 14:10 NIV).

I can't say I'm a fan of Woody Allen. It is somewhat coincidental that I offer another quote of his. He does say some funny things. I like this one: "I'm not afraid of death; I just don't what to be there when it happens."

> The boys in the class found it laughable
> Fearing God most of all seemed impractical.
> Love God first and foremost,
> Your neighbor to the utmost,
> And that, you will find quite fantastical!

You Oughta Be on Stage!

Jesus said first to his disciples, "Be on guard against the yeast of the Pharisees—I mean their hypocrisy. Whatever is covered up will be uncovered, and every secret will be made known. So then, whatever you have said in the dark will be heard in broad daylight, and whatever you have whispered in private in a closed room will be shouted from the housetops.

—Luke 12:1–3 (GNT)

"Aw-haw-haw! Gee! Ed, y'ought to be on the stage!" This was the caption for a cartoon published in *Life Magazine* circa 1924.

For several years, I was on stage as an amateur actor involved in many community theater productions. I enjoyed stepping out of my skin and playing the part of a different person. I was pretending to be someone I was not. This leads us to the origins of our English word *hypocrite*, which comes from the Greek word for actor or stage player, meaning *an interpreter from underneath*. Though I never wore a mask in community theater, actors in ancient Greek theater wore large masks to mark the character they were playing, so they interpreted the story from underneath their masks. The Greek word took on an extended meaning to refer to any person wearing a figurative mask and pretending to be someone or something they were not.

It seems this is exactly what Jesus was chiding the Pharisees for: pretending to be something they were not. But sooner or later the mask will come off, and their true nature will be revealed.

"All the world's a stage," Shakespeare wrote in his comedy, *As You Like It*. The speech compares the world to a stage and life to a play. We are all involved in the drama of life one could say. The question is, how are we going to play our part? In another play Shakespeare

31

wrote, "To thine own self be true." In other words, act in a way that agrees with one's beliefs and values. For the Christian, Martin Luther claimed that we are to be "little Christs."

Martin Luther used the image of the face mask not to denote that we are hypocrites, but quite the opposite: to talk about how God is at work in our lives. Luther's understanding of God's loving providence is that, rather than intervening in our daily lives directly, God chooses to act by working through earthly structures, including human agents, which he describes as *masks of God*. For example, in the Lord's Prayer, we pray, "Give us this day our daily bread." God responds to this prayer through the work of farmers, bakers, and merchants, among others. Those who fill these roles are not acting for themselves, but are acting as God's representatives, or *masks*, to meet our needs.

We may get a kick out of Jesus raking the Pharisees over the coals for their hypocrisy, their mask wearing, their pretending to be something they were not. Christians are often criticized by the world and even by fellow Christians for being hypocrites. Perhaps there is some truth to that indictment. How often do we put on a figurative mask to make it appear we are less of a sinner or even better than someone else?

May this passage from Luke challenge us to be God's *mask wearers* in the positive sense, to be the masks of God behind which God wants to remain concealed, and at the same time, revealed in and through us to accomplish His will and purpose, representing God's loving care for the world that He has made—yes—to live up to our true nature of being *little Christs*.

> The Pharisees wore pious masks
> Which Jesus took them to task,
> What you conceal
> Will be the reveal,
> In truthfulness strive to bask.

SNAKES IN THE GRASS

Crowds of people came out to John to be baptized by him.
"You snakes!" he said to them. "Who told you that you
could escape from the punishment God is about to send?
—Luke 3:7 (GNT)

This one always cracks me up. I can hardly contain myself when I hear or read it. John sees the religious elite coming to be baptized. Instead of welcoming them, what does he do? He insults them, calling them a bunch of slithering snakes! (Other translations use the term brood of vipers.) Wow! What did they do to deserve that?

Actually, it's what they *didn't* do: repent. The Jewish highbrows thought by claiming ancestry to their great patriarchal father, Abraham, that they could escape the consequences of their sinful lives without changing their behavior—without repentance. Extending the metaphor by referring to them as a tree that fails to produce good fruit, John warns them that God's ax is ready to cut them down and throw them into the fire. Some pretty hot words!

Apparently, that got the attention of a lot of folks in the crowd who thus asked, "What are we to do?" In the verses following, John gives some specific suggestions. (You can look that up for yourself.) Not only John, but Jesus also frequently attacked the religious phonies for their hypocrisy and declared, "Repent!"

Repentance. The great reformer Martin Luther, in his famous *Ninety-five Theses*, wrote as thesis number one: "When our Lord and Master Jesus Christ said, 'Repent,' [Matthew 4:17], he willed the entire life of believers to be one of repentance." What did he mean by that?

33

The Christian life is a daily, continual process of turning from our self-indulgent, wayward ways to turning back to God. The apostle Paul wrote in Romans 6, "We were buried therefore with Him by baptism into death, so that as Christ was raised from the dead by the glory of the Father, we too might walk in newness of life."

Luther, explaining this passage, writes in his *Small Catechism*, "Our sinful self, with all its evil deeds and desires, should be drowned through daily repentance; and that day after day a new self should arise to live with God in righteousness and purity forever." Making that our daily routine certainly should keep us busy. Elsewhere in this book, I quoted Paul saying we need to "work out our salvation with fear and trembling" (Philippians 2:12).

All this serves to remind me that I'm never that far from hell. Although I am saved by God's grace alone, I can never take this gift for granted. For Jesus said, "To whom much is given, of him will much be required" (Luke 12:48).

Reflection: "Life's full of tricky snakes and ladders" (Morrissey).

John called them a bunch of snakes
For being religious fakes
Because of their heritage,
They thought they were privileged
And therefore could make no mistakes.

TAKEOUT, ANYONE?

Jesus replied, "They do not need to go away.
You give them something to eat."
—Matthew 14:16 (NIV)

It was getting rather late in the afternoon. There was a large crowd gathered, and Jesus was healing a lot of the sick. The disciples came to Jesus and said, "You know, Master, it's getting kind of late, you must be tired, and these folks are probably getting pretty hungry. Let's tell them we're done for the day and send them into town to buy some food for themselves."

In his usual fashion, Jesus turned the tables and said, "They don't have to leave; *you* give them something to eat."

While all four gospels have a slight variation of this event, all do agree that the disciples are startled by Jesus's reply in which He expects them to come up with a solution to the problem. I can imagine them thinking something like, *That's very funny, Master, got any more good jokes?*

Incredulously, they ask Jesus what He expects them to feed the people with, to the point of suggesting it would cost a small fortune to go into town to buy a carryout order for the hungering crowd. John's gospel mentions the young boy present with five barley loaves and a few fish, but of course, the disciples reason, it would be ludicrous to think that would be enough to feed this mob of people.

I'm sure Jesus, in all His infinite wisdom, had this all figured out from the get-go. But He turned it over to the disciples to see what *they* would do. I suspect that's probably the way Jesus responds to us when we go to Him with a request or a situation we feel we cannot manage on our own. Sure, He could instantly grant our request or resolve our problem, but perhaps He prefers we figure out our own solution first. Sort of like saying, "Look, I gave you a brain with fantastic abilities, now put it to use." That doesn't mean He doesn't care or doesn't want to help us. Quite the contrary, perhaps He wants this to become a learning situation and for us to grow through the experience, to become a better person in the long run.

I like to think of it as a kind of partnership with God in solving our own problems. I once read a placard that gave this advice: "Sitting and wishing won't improve our fate. The Lord provides the fishes, but we have to dig the bait." To me that means God expects us to do our part in achieving our own goals and solving our own problems.

Many years ago, I heard this definition of prayer: "Prayer is asking it of God, doing it with God, and accomplishing it for God." A pretty good definition! In other words, instead of praying *gimme prayers* ("Lord, give me this…"), perhaps we should pray, "Lord, how can we work together to accomplish this, for *Your* glory?"

There's that old saying, "The Lord helps those who help themselves." Now that is not in the Bible as people tend to assume. In fact, when it comes to our salvation, the Bible says quite the opposite, "But God demonstrates his own love for us in this: While we were still (helpless) sinners, Christ died for us" (Romans 5:8 NIV). The word *helpless* was inserted by me, the writer.

Now while we are helpless in accomplishing our own salvation, that doesn't mean we are helpless in general. Quite the contrary. In another place, Jesus states that we have the capacity to do even greater things than Him!

"Very truly I tell you, whoever believes in me will do the works I have been doing, and they will do even greater things than these, because I am going to the Father" (John 14:12 NIV). Wow! Isn't that quite astounding? The Son of God says His followers will do even greater things than Him!

In 1 Corinthians 3:9, Paul says, "For we are co-workers in God's service." To me that means we are not only coworkers with each other, but coworkers with God himself, to work out His will and purpose. Florence Nightingale, considered the mother of modern nursing, wrote, "To be a fellow worker with God is the highest inspiration of which we can conceive man capable."

Of course, we know how the story turned out. Jesus took the boy's loaves and fishes and miraculously multiplied them to feed the entire crowd, with leftovers to boot. Now isn't that just like Jesus? He goes beyond doing the bare minimum, giving much more than we would possibly ask for or imagine.

Jesus said, "You (the disciples) give them something to eat." And they did—in partnership with Jesus. Together, they accomplished something great! And so can we!

> The crowd needed something to eat.
> To feed them would be quite a feat.
> With two fish and bread
> The Lord made a spread,
> With leftovers—now that was a treat!

Whatchu Talkin About, Jesus?

> The teachers of the Law and the chief priests tried
> to arrest Jesus on the spot, because they knew that
> he had told this parable against them…
> —Luke 20:19 (GNT)

The expression came from the popular eighties TV sitcom, *Different Strokes*. When Arnold Jackson didn't understand what his older brother, Willis, was saying, Arnold asked, "Whatchu talkin' about Willis?" The expression simply means *I did not understand what you're saying*. In a more sarcastic way, it also could imply the person is nonsensical, or doesn't know what he's saying.

Jesus had just finished telling the parable of the corrupt tenants in the vineyard. The account also is found in Matthew 21:33–46 and Mark 12:1–12. The story is an allegory based on another allegory in Isaiah 5:1–7, "The Song of the Vineyard." A landowner plants a vineyard on a very fertile hill. He dug the soil, cleared it of stones, planted the finest vines, built a tower to protect them, dug a pit, and waited for the grapes to ripen, but every grape was sour.

Jesus's spin-off story is about a vineyard owner who had rent out the vineyard to some farmers while he was away. When it came time for the harvest, the corrupt farmers beat up and drove away the men whom the owner sent to collect the profits. This seemed to repeat itself several times. Finally, the exasperated owner sent his own son to resolve the matter, thinking the tenants certainly would respect him. On the contrary, the treacherous farmers plotted to take over the vineyard for themselves and murdered the son. In retaliation, the owner would kill the wicked tenants and rent out the vineyard to other tenants. Explaining the object of the story, Jesus quoted Psalm

118:22, "The stone which the builders rejected turned out to be in the most important of all (the cornerstone)."

It seems the chief priests and the other religious leaders who were listening started to catch on and had one of those *aha* moments, when the light bulb comes on, as it dawned on them that the corrupt tenants in the story was a reference to them! With the mindset of Arnold Jackson, they may well have thought, *Whatchu talkin' about, Jesus?* In actuality, they knew all too well what Jesus was talking about, and so they hoped they could arrest and silence Jesus on the spot. However, because of Jesus's popularity, they feared the crowd might turn on them and end up with a riot on their hands.

So instead, the jealous religious elite tried to trap Jesus again by hatching a plot in which it would appear Jesus was acting in a treasonous way so that the Roman governor would have grounds to arrest him. This then led to the account of whether it is within Jewish law to pay taxes to the Roman emperor. You probably know the story already, but you can refresh your memory by reading the account in Matthew 22, Mark 12, or Luke 20.

Remember Aesop's fable of the fox and the sour grapes? A hungry fox goes into a luscious vineyard and tries to help himself to some grapes. But try as he might, he can't reach high enough to get them. So he concludes the grapes must be sour anyway. The moral is we tend to hate what we can't have.

Now you may be thinking, what's so funny about this parable of the wicked tenants? It doesn't exactly have a happy ending! What's so amusing is that try as they might, the chief priests and the religious elite simply could not bring Jesus down. Jesus was always one step ahead of them and was on to their evil plotting. After each failed encounter, I can envision these guys walking away with their tails between their legs thinking, *Rats, he got us again!* (Actually, I was thinking of a stronger word than rats, but we'll leave it at that.)

The Jewish leaders had an attitude like the fox and the sour grapes. The difference is, God was *giving* them the grapes—His kingdom, embodied in His own beloved Son. But throughout their long history, they continually turned away from God and rejected Him, with the mindset, "The grapes must be sour anyway."

I walk away from Jesus's parable having learned a few things. (After all, isn't that the intent of these stories?) Don't we, at all times have, a *sour grapes* attitude toward God? We think God doesn't love us, doesn't care for us. We don't have what we want, or we don't get what we want, so we say, "Forget it. It wasn't worth it in the first place." Sour grapes.

Like the religious scholars who tried to trip Jesus up, it just goes to show you can't outsmart, defeat, bamboozle, or pull one over on God. Instead, wouldn't it be in our best interests and simply easier just to trust and follow Him? Why keep trying to go up and down the staircase?

God truly desires that we be a part of His vineyard—His kingdom. In the Lord's Prayer, we pray, "Thy kingdom come." What does this mean? To answer that, Martin Luther explains in his *Small Catechism*, "The kingdom of God certainly comes by itself without our prayer, but we pray in this petition that it may come to us also."

Jesus said, "Do not be afraid, little flock, for it is your Father's good pleasure to give you the kingdom" (Luke 12:32 NRSV). Also, we read in 1 Corinthians 1:9 (GNT), "God is to be trusted, the God who called you to have fellowship with his Son, Jesus Christ our Lord." Words to live by!

A bunch of treacherous farm hands,
Plotted to seize the farm land.
The heir and son they slayed,
They thought they had it made.
In the end, it proved not so grand.

Handwriting in the Sand

They were trying to trap him into saying something
they could use against him, but Jesus stooped
down and wrote in the dust with his finger.

—John 8:6 (TLB)

The religious big wheels were at it again, trying to trap Jesus in order to accuse him of something to get him in trouble with the Roman government. They just wouldn't give up, even after all their failed attempts. You have to admire them for the tenacity. This time they wanted to bring charges against a prostitute, seeing if Jesus would uphold the Jewish law of stoning her to death for her wayward living. If you're interested, you can read about it in Leviticus 20:10.

So what does Jesus do? He takes His finger and starts writing in the sand. You've heard the expression, "The handwriting was on the wall." It usually means something bad is about to happen. The original version comes from Daniel 5:5. A human hand appears and begins writing on the wall of Belshazzar's palace. It turned out to be a prediction of the fall of Belshazzar's kingdom. I suppose there's no known connection; however, I wonder if Jesus might have had that image in his mind when he started writing on the ground? With God, you never can tell, right?

So what does Jesus write? We don't know. John doesn't bother to tell us. Nor do the other gospel writers include this incident in their gospels. Maybe they were off on another assignment. One commentary suggests that Jesus was drawing pictures in the sand. Perhaps. But that's probably not important. What is important is what Jesus says.

During this whole process, the religious leaders were peppering Jesus with questions while His finger was busy at work in the sand. John doesn't tell us what they asked. Finally, Jesus pauses, looks up, and says, "Whichever one of you has never committed a sin, let him be the one to throw the first stone."

Now there are different versions of that depending on what English translation you choose. However, I can't help wondering if the underlying message under that question wasn't, "How many of *you* slept with her last week?" Well, that certainly cuts to the chase, doesn't it?

Foiled again. Silence falls and so do the stones. Everyone vacates the scene except Jesus and the woman. He lovingly says, "All your accusers are gone and I don't condemn you either. Go, but do not sin again." End of story. Hmm... I still wonder what he was drawing in the sand.

They ushered in the prostitute,
The Pharisees in hot pursuit.
As Jesus wrote into the ground
No perfect saints could thus be found,
With that, no one to prosecute.

EVERYBODY'S OUT TO GET ME!

He (Elijah) replied, "I have worked very hard for the Lord God of
the heavens; but the people of Israel have broken their covenant
with you and torn down your altars and killed your prophets,
and only I am left; and now they are trying to kill me too.
—1 Kings 19:10 (TLB)

Poor Elijah. He's having a rough time. As I read this account, an
old song from the popular TV program *Hew Haw* came to mind:
"Gloom, despair, and agony on me; deep, dark depression, excessive
misery. If it weren't for bad luck, I'd have no luck at all. Gloom,
despair, and agony on me." I am amused by Elijah's words because
he is so *human*.

Don't we all feel that way at times, indulging in our own little
pity party? When everything seems to be going against us, we turn
inward on ourselves and think everybody's out to get us. We stand in
good company. The prophet Elijah felt the same way.

After Elijah slaughtered the prophets of Baal, Queen Jezebel
vowed to kill him. Since they didn't have the witness protection program back then—at least I don't think they did—he fled for his life.
I guess I might have done the same thing. Being physically, emo-
tionally, and spiritually drained, Elijah literally wanted to die. He
despaired over his fellow countrymen turning from God to worship
Baal. He wondered why God had failed him. Elijah worked so hard
to bring the people to repentance. Elijah's faith and self-respect were
at their lowest. Eventually he declared, "I've had it," he told God.
"Take my life."

Elijah's attitude kind of reflects that old children's poem about
eating the worms: "Nobody likes me, everybody hates me, guess I'll

go eat worms. Long, thin, slimy ones; short, fat, juicy ones, itsy, bitsy fuzzy wuzzy worms."

Of course, God didn't give into Elijah's death wish. In fact, God didn't seem to be too sympathetic at all. In essence, He said, "Get off the pity pot and get back to work. I'm not done with you yet. You're not alone as you think you are. There are still over seven thousand men in Israel who have not bowed to Baal. Now do what I tell you." I would guess that's not exactly what Elijah wanted to hear.

Eventually Elijah regained his faith and his strength and completed the work God had set out for him. He learned that his perceived failure was not a failure at all. God did not forsake Elijah, letting him stew in his own juice. God simply had a different plan and a better idea which, ultimately, Elijah would come to realize. Maybe that's something we need to keep in mind.

Robert Schuller, the late TV religious icon, wrote a book called *Success Is Never Ending, Failure Is Never Final.* Schuller said, "Success is the journey, not the destination. Therefore, success is unending and failure is never final. A bend in the road is not the end of the road." Great stuff. Wish I had thought of it.

Elijah had so much to dread,
Queen Jezebel wanted him dead!
He fussed and he sniveled,
His faith had quite dwindled,
but God simply said forge ahead.

Parable of the Linen Shorts

The LORD told me to go and buy myself some linen shorts and to put them on; but he told me not to put them in water. So I bought them and put them on. Then the LORD spoke to me again and said, "Go to the Euphrates River and hide the shorts in a hole in the rocks." So I went and hid them near the Euphrates. Some time later the LORD told me to go back to the Euphrates and get the shorts. So I went back, and when I found the place where I had hidden them, I saw that they were ruined and were no longer any good. Then the LORD spoke to me again. He said, "This is how I will destroy the pride of Judah and the great pride of Jerusalem. These evil people have refused to obey me. They have been as stubborn and wicked as ever, and have worshiped and served other gods. So then, they will become like these shorts that are no longer any good. Just as shorts fit tightly around the waist, so I intended all the people of Israel and Judah to hold tightly to me. I did this so that they would be my people and would bring praise and honor to my name; but they would not obey me."
—Jeremiah 13:1–11 (GNT)

You have to admit God uses some pretty strange metaphors. He tells the prophet Jeremiah to buy some linen shorts, put them on, and then hide them in a cave. Go back after a long time and retrieve them, which, when Jeremiah did, he found the shorts to be rotten and useless.

Now what's the point of all this? Another translation uses the term waistcloth. Essentially, it was a loincloth. The message was this—Israel had become like a rotten piece of underwear! In pride, Israel had refused to obey God's Word, following their own wanton ways, worshipping their self-made gods, and abandoning the only true God. So God was fed up with them and ready to throw them in the trash like dirty underwear.

This is not the first time we see the image of a linen short or waistcloth. In Leviticus 16:4, we read that before Aaron could enter the Holy of Holies on the Day of Atonement, he had to don himself with the sacred linen tunic, with linen undergarments next to his body. He is to tie the linen sash around him and put on the linen turban. These were what we today would call his holy vestments.

It wasn't unusual for God to command the prophets to do some pretty peculiar behaviors to tell of a forewarning or to illustrate a point. Isaiah was told to take off his clothes and sandals and walk around naked for three years as a warning to the Egyptians and Ethiopians (Isaiah 20:1–6). Isn't that a little bizarre?

Ezekiel was told to take a brick and draw a relief map of Jerusalem with a model of a military attack to illustrate the impending fall of the city. Then he was to take an iron plate and place it between himself and the city, symbolizing an iron wall. As if playing a Nintendo video game, he was to be the attacker and the city the target. (It appears they had virtual war games even back then.)

Years ago, a friend told me his mother advised him to always wear clean underwear in case he was in an accident and had to go to the hospital. He wouldn't want to be caught with dirty underwear on! I don't think God is too concerned about the condition of our underwear as he is our innerwear and giving him first place in our lives. In that way, on the Day of Judgment, we won't be caught with any *spiritual dirty underwear*. How's that for a metaphor?

The prophet Jeremiah tells a parable:
His countrymen were quite unbearable.
Like underwear that's been soiled,
Their character was quite spoiled,
The consequences irreversible.

If God Loves Me So Much,
Why Is This Happening to Me?

Gideon said to him, "If I may ask, sir, why has all this happened
to us if the LORD is with us? What happened to all the wonderful
things that our fathers told us the LORD used to do—how he
brought them out of Egypt? The LORD has abandoned us and
left us to the mercy of the Midianites." Then the LORD ordered
him, "Go with all your great strength and rescue Israel from the
Midianites. I myself am sending you." Gideon replied, "But Lord,
how can I rescue Israel? My clan is the weakest in the tribe of
Manasseh, and I am the least important member of my family."
The LORD answered, "You can do it because I will help you. You
will crush the Midianites as easily as if they were only one man."
Gideon replied, "If you are pleased with me, give me some proof
that you are really the LORD. Please do not leave until I bring you
an offering of food." He said, "I will stay until you come back."
—Judges 6:13–18 (GNT)

You've heard of Gideon. Besides his name being used by a certain
Bible distribution organization, he's the guy in the Old Testament
who did some fleecing. Oh no, not the corrupt kind of ripping people off. I'm talking about putting out a fleece. Essentially, he put God
to a small test to see if He would do what He promised. Gideon put a
piece of wool on the ground and asked that the morning dew be only
on the wool but not on the ground. That's what happened. Pushing
his luck a little bit, he asked God for one more test. This time, it
would be to let the wool be dry and the ground wet. Again, that's

what happened. Now all this came about after the dialogue that took place in the above passage.

I chuckled when I heard this because I could detect the cynicism in Gideon's voice. If God is with us, why in the heck are we having so much trouble? Aren't we all like Gideon? When a perceived misfortune strikes or we're just having a bad day, we lay the blame on God and ask the same question, "If God loves me so much, why is all this happening?" It seems like a plausible question, but it's full of holes. Look at the biblical account.

The Israelites were being harassed by the Midianites and other neighboring enemies. Why? The writer explains that although God rescued them from the Egyptians and gave them the promised land, still the Israelites abandoned God and worshipped the gods of their pagan neighbors. Now an angel appears to Gideon and says, "The Lord is with you." That's when Gideon askes the mocking question, "If God is with us, why are we having all this calamity?"

What's funny is the angel doesn't go for the bait to argue with him. Instead the angel simply declares that Gideon has been chosen to overthrow the Midianites. Now Gideon is really taken aback. The story goes on to show how all that came about, but that seems to be straying from the point of the original subject.

When we either genuinely or mockingly ask God why some adversity has befallen us, we are, like Gideon, ignoring God's love and goodness and, in effect, blaming God. We disregard the fact that like Adam and Eve, we are rebels—sinners on the run. We question God's love, doubt God's goodness, and dismiss God's providence.

When you think about it, isn't it true that much of the time *we* are the cause of our own misfortunes and negative circumstances? We make dumb choices and decisions, and then wonder, *Gee, why is this happening?* Or maybe, like the apostle Paul, we know what is right, but do the wrong anyway (Romans 7:19). Or maybe in our self-centered spirit of rugged individualism, we feel we can go it alone without needing God or anyone else to guide us or assist us—the idea, "I don't need anyone, not even God."

Of course, there is the underlying fact that we do live in a sinful and fallen world in which we are the casualties of other people's sin and bad choices. We know it's true: bad things do happen to good (albeit, still sinful) people. There really is a devil whom Paul calls the god of this world (2 Corinthians 4:4) who tries to frustrate all people from seeing the light of the gospel that shines in the glory of Jesus.

So instead of imitating Gideon's disposition to accuse God of a lack of love and blaming God for our troubles, we would do well to hearken to the promise of our Lord, "I will be with you always to the end of the age" (Matthew 28:20). Yes, bad things happen to us sometimes, and it's no one's fault, not even our own. God is there for those times also.

Also, consider the admonition of Paul in Romans 8, which talks about living in the spirit of Christ. If we are controlled by our lower sinful nature which is against God, we cannot please God, and, in effect, we are blazing the trail of our own demise. However, if we live with the spirit of Christ within us, even though our physical bodies will die, yet we shall live by the same spirit that raised Jesus from the dead (Romans 8:12–13). Finally, we have these reassuring words of Paul in Romans 8, "If God is for us, who can be against us? I am certain that there is nothing in all creation that will be able to separate us from God's love in Christ Jesus."

So getting back to the original story, what happened to Gideon? God stayed with him, and he did defeat the Midianites. The fleecing thing was to be a sign to Gideon that God would be true to His word. It's quite an intriguing story. Gideon and his army of a mere one hundred men attacked with torches hidden in clay jars, so the enemy wouldn't see them. At Gideon's command, the warriors broke the jars for the torches to shine, blew their trumpets, and God made the enemy soldiers attack one another! You can read all about it in Judges 6–7. You just may end up laughing.

No time for tea and crumpets,
Pursue the Midianite muppets!
With a scant hundred men
Gideon's army did then
Beat the foe with mere jars and trumpets!

FOOD TO GAG A MAGGOT!

> The people lost their patience and spoke against God and Moses.
> They complained, "Why did you bring us out of Egypt to die in
> this desert, where there is no food or water? We can't stand any
> more of this miserable food!" Then the LORD sent poisonous snakes
> among the people, and many Israelites were bitten and died."
> —Numbers 21:4–6 (GNT)

I heard this passage read in church yesterday, the fourth Sunday in
Lent. It was part of a larger sequence of the Israelite's wandering in
the wilderness on the way to the promised land. Of course, I couldn't
help but to snicker when it came to the part of the bellyaching about
the food (pun intended).

The Israelites were at it again. Complain, complain, complain.
This time, they were carping about the manna God had provided
to sustain them. Some of the English translations to describe their
assessment of the food are quite amusing: worthless food, miserable
food, wretched food, miserable stuff, awful food, terrible food, and
the list goes on. This account carries me back to my high school days,
when a friend, commenting on the lunch menu served in the school
cafeteria, jested, "This food could gag a maggot off a gut wagon!" (I'll
let you look up what a gut wagon is—there really is such a thing.)

However, God remedied the upheaval in short order. He sent a
batch of poisonous snakes to deaden the whiners—literally! However,
the situation was not a total debacle. To redeem their plight, God
instructed Moses to make a bronze snake and put it on a pole, so that
anyone who had been bitten could look at the snake and be healed.

The gospel writer John picked up on this and drew an analogy
between the snake on the pole and Jesus on the cross, saying that

whoever believes in Him will have eternal life. That leads into the verse which is sometimes called the *gospel in a nutshell*, "For God so loved the world that he gave his only Son, so that everyone who believes in him may not perish but may have eternal life" (John 3:16 NRSV).

From this account of the Israelites griping about the manna, I've come away with two insights. One, it's okay to complain to God—the psalm writers did it all the time. See Psalm 64:1 (NIV) for example. Just show some respect. I'm guessing you don't want to bring on any snakes. Two, before you complain about the taste of your food, think of someone who has nothing to eat.

> The Hebrews were always complaining;
> They thought of the food quite disdaining.
> Killer snakes God then sent,
> But then He did relent;
> A snake on a pole life sustaining.

THE PERSISTENT PROVOKER

> When the Devil finished tempting Jesus in
> every way, he left him for a while.
> —Luke 4:13 (GNT)

We could call him the bedeviling devil. Satan doesn't give up trying to persuade Jesus to give up His mission. You have to admit what the devil was offering was very tempting: food (after not eating for forty days), control over all the kingdoms of the world (Didn't Jesus already have that? See Psalm 24:1.), and protection from foolish decisions—jump off the cliff, the angels will protect you.

The devil should have known he was no match for the Lord of heaven and earth, but he kept on trying—gotta give him credit for that.

Finally, the exasperated Satan decides to give it a rest, but he hasn't given up completely. He never does! Perhaps he was thinking, *Maybe I lost this one battle, Jesus, but you haven't won the war. I'll be back. I'll get you later.*

That's exactly what Luke recorded. Some translations read, "He [Satan] departed from Him until an opportune time." I most like the wording of the GNT Bible: "He [Satan] left Him *for a while.*" Satan assured Jesus that he wasn't giving up so easily.

And of course, Satan did return multiple times, as in vain, he did his utmost to tempt Jesus to shirk His ministry and wriggle out of the cross. That would be the ultimate victory for Satan and all his dark and destructive powers.

We see the crushing force of Satan while Jesus was praying in the garden of Gethsemane, where again, Satan was trying to get Jesus to abandon the cross. The gospel writers record that Jesus was filled with grief and anguish, almost to the point of breaking Him, as He begged His Father to dodge the cross. Luke records that an angel came to strengthen Him, his distress was so great. Peter, James, and John saw beads of blood on Jesus that appeared like sweat. Twice Jesus exhorted His sleeping disciples to pray that they would not fall into temptation. Jesus knew the heavy hand of Satan was upon them all.

We fallible human beings certainly are no match for Satan on our own. Martin Luther addresses this in his great hymn "A Mighty Fortress." A portion of stanza one reads, "The old satanic foe has sworn to work us woe. With craft and dreadful might he arms himself to fight. On earth he has no equal."

It is no accident that this hymn is the appointed hymn of the day for the first Sunday in Lent. The temptation of Jesus in the wilderness is the gospel lesson for the day. Without quoting all four stanzas of the hymn (the reader is encouraged to read all the lyrics of the hymn), the message is that the devil and all the forces of darkness are hell-bent on our eternal destruction.

The apostle Paul elaborates on this in Ephesians 6:12 (NRSV), "For our struggle is not against enemies of blood and flesh, but against the rulers, against the authorities, against the cosmic powers of this present darkness, against the spiritual forces of evil in the heavenly places."

We may tend to think the devil is the opposite of God. Not so. God has no opposites because no one is equal to God. Light is not the opposite of darkness; darkness is simply the absence of light. Cold and heat are not opposites. Cold is simply the absence of heat. The devil certainly would have us believe that he is God's equal opposite—another one of Satan's lies.

Only Jesus can save us in this life or death struggle that Paul refers to in Ephesians 6:12. The truth is the victory has already been won and our salvation is secured through the cross and resurrection of our Lord. As Luther writes in the final stanza of "A Mighty Fortress, "...were they to take our house, goods, honor, child or spouse, through life be wrenched away, they cannot win the day. The Kingdom's ours forever!"

> The devil is very persistent
> On our doom he's quite insistent
> But Jesus is victorious;
> He wins redemption glorious!
> In Him we stand resistant.

POWER PLAY

Pilate therefore said to him, "Do you refuse to
speak to me? Do you not know that I have power
to release you, and power to crucify you?
—John 19:10 (NRSV)

This passage is enough to knock me off the organ bench with guffaws of laughter were it not for the fact that it is read during the solemnities of Holy Week. One might think there is nothing very amusing during such a somber and hallowed time. So then, what's so funny?

Jesus is on trial for His life. The exasperated Pontius Pilate is trying to save Jesus from the cross. He knows that the charges against Jesus are trumped up and that Jesus has really done nothing to merit the death penalty. Impatient with Jesus's lack of self-defense, Pilate blurts out, "Don't you know I have the power to release you and to crucify you?"

Think of the absurdity of it all; Pilate, this puny puppet governor stuck in the backwater province of the Roman empire, is telling the King of kings and Lord of lords, the Creator of the entire universe, the Almighty and eternal God, that he, Pilate, has power over Him! If Pilate only knew how ludicrous his statement was! It's a wonder Jesus Himself did not burst out laughing, were it not for the fact that by that time, He had gone all night without sleep or nourishment, had been bound in chains, beaten to a pulp, ridiculed and spit upon, and was facing the torture and agony of the cross. That would not put one in a very humorous mood. Instead, Jesus quietly answers, "You have no power over me except which has been given to you from heaven." That's it. Pilate caves in to the demand of the unruly crowd, and Jesus is led off to be crucified.

Of course, we know that Jesus could have used His almighty power to escape the cross. As He said earlier in the garden of Gethsemane, "Don't you know I could call upon my Father for help, and at once He would send me twelve armies of angels? But in that case, how could the Scriptures come true which say that this is what must happen?" (Matthew 26:53 GNT). Yes, Jesus could have given into the mockers who jeered, "You were going to tear down the Temple and build it back up in three days! Save yourself if you are God's Son! Come on down from the cross!" (Matthew 27:40 GNT). Thanks be to God that Jesus would have none of that and remained true to His purpose to save the world from sin and eternal damnation.

To much of the world today, the Gospel and the message of the cross are unbelievable legends and nonsense. Christians are regarded as gullible fools. Nothing new. This also was true in the early church as declared by Paul in 1 Corinthians 1:18, 23–24 (GNT):

> For the message about Christ's death on the cross is nonsense to those who are being lost; but for us who are being saved it is God's power. As for us, we proclaim the crucified Christ, a message that is offensive to the Jews and nonsense to the Gentiles; but for those whom God has called, both Jews and Gentiles, this message is Christ, who is the power of God and the wisdom of God.

Yes, Pontius Pilate, you did have the power to crucify the Lord of life or to set Him free, but only because it was given to you by the Lord Himself. In the Introduction, I affirmed how the crucifixion/resurrection is the watershed moment, the Himalayan event in all human history. John Bowering (1792–1872) summarized this so beautifully in his beloved hymn, "In the Cross of Christ I Glory."

> "In the cross of Christ I Glory
> Towering o'er the wrecks of time.
> All the light of sacred story
> Gathers round its head sublime."

Pilates' manner was quite lugubrious
His words to Jesus very ludicrous
The cross was Jesus' hour
To save us from sin's power
The light of the cross very luminous

THE LAST WORD

When Jesus had received the wine, he said, "It is finished."
Then he bowed his head and gave up his spirit.
—John 19:30 (NRSV)

An old hymn for Good Friday goes, "'Tis finished!' so the Savior cried, and meekly bowed His head and died; 'Tis finished—yes, the race is run, the battle fought, the victory won" (Samuel Stennett 1787).

What could possibly be funny or even remotely amusing about Good Friday? It was, after all, the darkest day in human history (Luke 23:44). The Lord of life had been savagely and innocently slain. The method of crucifixion was such a cruel and barbaric mode of capital punishment that the great Roman statesman and scholar, Marcus Tullius Cicero, said he hoped the time comes when the very memory of crucifixion will disappear from the minds of Roman citizenry; it is such a disgrace to Roman civilization. However, it wasn't until the early fourth century that Constantine the Great, the first Christian emperor, finally abolished crucifixion in the Roman Empire.

Though we don't think of Jesus's crucifixion as anything to bring joy, I am intrigued by the fact there are a few hymns written in praise and celebration of the event. One is titled, "We Sing the Praise of Him Who Died" says, "We sing the praise of Him who died, of Him who died upon the cross; the sinners' hope let men deride, for this we count the world but loss" (Thomas Kelly 1815).

Another hymn titled, "The Death of Jesus Christ, Our Lord" says, "The death of Jesus Christ, our Lord, we celebrate with one accord; It is our comfort in distress, our heart's sweet joy and happiness" (Haquin Spegel 1645–1714).

So how do we find *sweet joy and happiness* in Jesus's death on the cross? For one thing, Jesus Himself counted it as joy. We read in Hebrews 12:2, "... looking to Jesus the pioneer and perfecter of our faith, who for the sake of the joy that was set before him endured the cross..." We also find a clue in the second stanza of the above hymn, "The Death of Jesus Christ, Our Lord."

"He blotted out with His own blood, the judgment that against us stood; for us He full atonement made, and all our debt He fully paid."

The celebration is not for death, but of the life that Jesus brings through *His* death. When He exclaimed, "It is finished," it was a cry of completion and victory over sin, Satan, and over "the cosmic powers of this present darkness, against the spiritual forces of evil in the heavenly places" (Ephesians 6:12).

Referring back to the above hymn, "'Tis Finished," the final stanza reads, "'Tis finished! Let the joyful sound be heard through all the nations round; 'tis finished! Let the echo fly through heaven and hell, through earth and sky. Amen."

It is finished, Jesus cried,
As on the cross He died;
He is God's holy Son,
O'er darkness He has won,
Let us praise the Crucified!

THAT SCANDALOUS SIGN

Pilate also had an inscription written and put on the cross. It read, "Jesus of Nazareth, the King of the Jews." Many of the Jews read this inscription, because the place where Jesus was crucified was near the city; and it was written in Hebrew, in Latin, and in Greek.
—John 19:19–20 (NRVS)

The religious muckety-mucks were irate again. This time, they were mad at Pilate, not Jesus. Jesus was hanging on the cross, dead. That should have been enough to shut them up, but it wasn't. Now they had a beef with Pilate over the sign he erected over the cross, *Jesus of Nazareth, King of the Jews*.

The chief priests objected. "Don't write THAT! Instead, make it, 'This man *said* I am the King of the Jews.'"

Essentially, Pilate said, "Too late. I'm not changing anything; it stays exactly as it is!"

This certainly raises some questions. Why were the religious bigwigs annoyed with the sign, and why did Pilate nail it up in the first place? And why was it written in three different languages? To answer the first question, we know the religious leaders were jealous of Jesus's popularity and the great things He was doing. He called them out on their hypocrisy and challenged the status quo.

Who knows why Pilate wrote the sign? Perhaps it was because the leaders told Pilate Jesus was claiming Himself as the Messiah, a king (Luke 23:2). But when Pilate asked Jesus if He was a king, He remained silent. In John's gospel, Jesus declares His kingdom is not of this world (John 18:36). Pilate simply acted on the assumption.

But why is the sign in three languages? Perhaps it was Pilate's way of mocking the bloodthirsty mob demanding the crucifixion.

Maybe it was a warning: this is what will happen to you if you break the law. The place of the crucifixion also was near the city where people of all three spoken languages might pass through. That's the simplest explanation.

However, on a deeper level, it could very well have been part of God's holy plan. This is where the wry, amusing part comes in. My guess is God used the sign—this object of derision and ridicule—and transformed it into a glorious proclamation: to proclaim that Jesus, in fact, is the King. Not just King of the Jews. The King of all creation, of all time. The servant King who came to redeem the world (John 3:16). Pontius Pilate, that insignificant puppet of the Roman emperor in the tiny boondocks of Palestine, was in fact an instrument of God in spreading the Gospel! Just maybe, that's why, in fact, the sign was inscribed in all three of the world's languages, for all to get the message! Now doesn't that just make you want to laugh?

The sign read Jesus the King;
For the Jews it caused quite a sting.
By holy design, He's Lord of all time
His praises now let us sing!

THE LAST LAUGH

The women ran from the tomb, badly frightened,
but also filled with joy, and rushed to find the
disciples to give them the angel's message.
—Matthew 28:8 (TLB)

"Hallelujah! He is risen! He is risen indeed! Hallelujah!" (Luke 24:34).
That is the joyful proclamation resounding throughout Christendom
on Easter Sunday, the resurrection of our Lord.

This magnificent Easter hymn sums it up so well, "The Strife Is
O'er, the Battle Done."

"The strife is o'er the battle done; now is the victor's triumph
won; now be the song of praise begun. Alleluia! The powers of death
have done their worst, but Christ their legions hath dispersed. Let
shouts of holy joy outburst. Alleluia!" (origin: Latin hymn, seven-
teenth century; English translation, Francis Pott 1859).

Amid the joy and celebration of Easter, there is a part of the
story that's not exactly complimentary to Jesus's followers. The irony
is, it was the enemies of Jesus, not his followers, who were the first
to believe in the resurrection. Matthew reports that after the angel
rolled away the stone from the tomb, the guards were so flabber-
gasted by the event, they ran into town to tell the Jewish leaders
what took place. That is odd in itself because if a Roman soldier
abandoned his post, it would have resulted in certain death as a punishment. Nevertheless, the soldiers left anyway. The chief priests and
the elders decided to hatch a plot to make the resurrection out to be
a hoax and a lie. So they gave the Roman guards hush money and
promised to protect them from Pilate for abandoning their post and

to say the disciples came by at night and stole Jesus's body when they fell asleep. You have to admit, they cooked up quite a tale!

And a tale is all it is! The empty tomb still remains an unwavering and certain witness of the resurrection, beckoning even the most critical skeptic to examine the evidence supporting the absolute truth of the resurrection, for which there is overwhelming physical and historic validation.

The good news is the disciples and the women and even Doubting Thomas did affirm the truth of the Risen Christ, and so believers down through the ages have exclaimed, "He is risen, Hallelujah!" The apostle Paul sums this up so well in 1 Corinthians 15 (NRSV), which appears to be an early creed of the starting church:

> For I handed on to you as of first importance what I in turn had received: that Christ died for our sins in accordance with the scriptures, and that he was buried, and that he was raised on the third day in accordance with the Scriptures, and that he appeared to Cephas, then to the twelve. Then he appeared to more than five hundred brothers and sisters at one time, most of whom are still alive, though some have died. Then he appeared to James, then to all the apostles. Last of all, as to one untimely born, he appeared also to me.

On Good Friday, Jesus had the last word. "It is finished!" On Easter Sunday, as the stone was rolled away from the tomb and He arose victoriously, Jesus truly had the last laugh!

On Easter morn Jesus' foes
A hoax, they tried to impose.
The guards were paid cash
To lie unabashed
That Jesus, in fact, arose!

CAFETERIA RELIGION

So Paul took his stand in the open space at the Areopagus
and laid it out for them. "It is plain to see that you Athenians
take your religion seriously. When I arrived here the other
day, I was fascinated with all the shrines I came across.
And then I found one inscribed, TO THE GOD NOBODY
KNOWS. I'm here to introduce you to this God so you can
worship intelligently, know who you're dealing with."

—Acts 17:23 (MSG)

In the book of Acts, the apostle Paul is visiting Athens. He observed
the Athenians were very religious, or, as we might say today, *spiritual.*
There were all kinds of religious altars set up including one *to an
unknown God. The Message* paraphrases and translates it, "TO THE
GOD NOBODY KNOWS." I kind of think of it as, *To the nobody god.*

We see the same kind of thing today. Instead of many physical
religious altars set up, we find a plethora of self-made religiosities
under the umbrella of "spiritualism." I frequently hear someone say,
"I don't go to church, or I'm not religious, but I am *spiritual.*" In
place of embracing any particular religion or doctrine, the person
concocts their own belief system by extracting a cluster of nebulous
concepts and ideas from a combination of religions, philosophies,
and ideologies, and calling themselves "spiritual." I think of it as cafeteria-style religion.

This reminds me of a song I heard as a kid. It went, "You take
your road and I'll take mine and we'll all get to heaven at the very
same time. The ladder doesn't matter, it's the way that you climb, so
we'll all get to heaven at the very same time."

It seems like a cute little jingle. I suppose conventional wisdom would agree with it. In reality, the only thing true about the song is affirming the existence of heaven. The rest of the song is total deception and hogwash. Popular belief depicts heaven as some kind of fairy tale-like never-never land, to which all roads lead and to which all achieve by climbing some sort of metaphorical ladder. You strive and struggle, you may miss a wrung or two, but if you're lucky, you'll get there.

In sharp contrast, the Christian gospel affirms heaven is a real habitation given as a gift to those who are believers in and followers of the Lord Jesus Christ—the one who declared, "I am the Road, also the Truth, and also the Life" (John 14:6 MSG). Jesus did not say that out of arrogance, but out of love, as he "desires that everyone be saved and come to the knowledge of the truth" (1 Timothy 2:4 NRSV). Read it also from *The Message* paraphrase:

> He wants not only us but *everyone* saved, you know, everyone to get to know the truth *we've* learned: that there's one God and only one, and one Priest-Mediator between God and us—Jesus, who offered himself in exchange for everyone held captive by sin, to set them all free.

This cafeteria-style religion is characteristic of the age of postmodernism in which we live. Postmodernism declares there is no real truth, that all knowledge is made or invented, and certainly not revealed. So you say you are *spiritual*. What does that mean? Even Satan is spiritual. Remember, he quoted the Bible to Jesus! (Matthew 4). I often think it would be great if Christians knew the Bible as well as the devil.

The followers who worship the devil are spiritual also. The Taliban is spiritual. There are a host of religions and sects who engage in every depravity known to man and yet would call themselves spiritual. Does anyone aspire to *that* kind of spirituality?

As Paul was in Athens, he could see the people there were very spiritual, with a host of religious shrines including one honoring the god nobody knows. He explains to them that this god is really the one true God of heaven and earth, revealed in the person of Jesus Christ.

So you're spiritual? Great! So is everyone. It's part of your DNA from your Creator. Be specific. A father was helping his son with his math homework. It became apparent the boy was less enthusiastic about doing multiple problems connected to the same concept.

"I've got it, Dad!" the son declared, hoping Dad would let him out of doing all the assignment.

Seeing a teaching moment, the father explained that a concept is just a concept until you learn how to work it out in *practice*. The apostle Paul wrote about practice to his friends in Philippi, "Put into practice what you learned and received from me" (Philippians 4:9 GNT).

You're spiritual. Give it substance, not by designing your own spirituality, cafeteria style. Consign your spirituality to that which is ultimate truth, to that which is solid, real, and eternal—to the God whom Paul introduced to the Athenians, "This God you can worship intelligently and know who you're dealing with"—yes, JESUS, the way, the truth, and the life.

Those words—the way, the truth, and the life—were spoken by Jesus in reference to Himself, to which he added, "No one comes to the Father except through me." Jesus said that in reply to Thomas's question, "Lord, we don't know where you are going, so how can we know the way?" (John 14:5–6). Remember Thomas? Sometimes referred to as Doubting Thomas. Thomas was a pessimist and a realist, inquisitive, honest, human. After touching Jesus's nail-scarred hands, feet, and pierced side, Thomas, convinced of Jesus's resurrection, cried, "My Lord and my God!" (John 20:28).

Isn't there a little bit of Thomas in all of us? Doubting but wanting to believe? Maybe even pessimistic at times? Inquisitive, honest (hopefully), and yes, very human? The apostles knew Jesus was who he claimed to be: God. "Whoever has seen me (Jesus) has seen the Father," Jesus assured them (John 14:9). The apostles who were martyred did not die for a lie. They went to their deaths proclaiming

Jesus Christ crucified and risen because they knew it was true. They were eye witnesses.

> In his disciples' presence Jesus performed many other miracles which are not written down in this book. But these have been written in order that you may believe that Jesus is the Messiah, the Son of God, and that through your faith in him you may have life. (John 20:30–31 GNT)

Those words invite us to abandon any cafeteria-style religion and to entrust our lives to the Gospel, that we indeed may "have life in His name."

> "I'm spiritual," the person claims;
> Religions are all the same;
> But Jesus, alone, for sin did atone.
> Salvation by no other name!

Gospel or Garbage?

Yes, everything else is worthless when compared with
the infinite value of knowing Christ Jesus my Lord.
For his sake I have discarded everything else, counting
it all as garbage, so that I could gain Christ.

—Philippians 3:8 (NLT)

Ever have to take out the garbage? Not a fun job. Probably one of the lowliest tasks one could be called upon to do. It's dirty, ugly, stinky—just plain gross. In my house we try to recycle as much as possible. Nevertheless, there's still garbage. Eggshells, potato peelings, coffee grounds, banana skins, maybe even some rotten meat that got forgotten in the fridge. Yuck! Also, in my house, we have a menagerie of cats who use a litter box. And the remains of that litter box need to be put into a plastic bag and discarded also. I doubt if there is anything raunchier than a bag of dirty cat litter! (Yes, it's my job to take care of that also.)

I chuckle at some of the other English translations used in this passage for the word *garbage*. Those include, *rubbish, trash, worthless trash, filth,* and some get even more graphic and use the words *dung* and *excrement*—yes, poop! That's very akin to dirty cat litter! The original Greek uses the word (in English) *skyvala*. The closest translation is *refuse* or *rubbish*.

A seminary professor gave each student in his class a sheet of paper. On it, he told them to write down everything that was most valuable and most important to them. At the conclusion of the exercise, the professor gathered up all the papers and threw them in the trash while quoting this passage from Philippians 3:8. Wow!

As I reflect on this passage, I think of a mountain of steaming, smelly garbage in a huge landfill, fermenting in the sun, with seagulls swooping down to grab a free meal. Now isn't that a pretty picture?

Paul's point is easy to grasp. He considers everything—yes, everything—to be garbage, trash, excrement, in comparison to knowing Jesus as Lord. Hmmm…wouldn't that cause one to make some priority reassessments?

Let Jesus be your treasure,
Your source of greatest pleasure.
Paul's gain he counted as loss,
Self-glory nailed to the cross,
In Christ we know joy beyond measure!

THE LAST SHOT

> For you yourselves know very well that the day of the Lord will come like a thief in the night. For God has destined us not for wrath but for obtaining salvation through our Lord Jesus Christ.
>
> —1 Thessalonians 5:2, 9 (NRSV)

In most books, this is called the epilogue, the author's parting words. I like to think of it as *the last shot*.

The world was in the throes of the coronavirus pandemic. It was 3:25 a.m. when the power went off. I looked out the window, and all I could see was total darkness with complete silence. It was very eerie. My imagination went into overdrive. I began to wonder, is this the "day of the Lord?" (1 Thessalonians 5:2). Seriously, I listened for the sound of the great trumpet, the sky lighting up in a blaze of glory, the voice of the archangel, and the Lord Himself coming down from heaven for the great judgment! (1 Thessalonians 4:16).

As a lifelong Christian, I've taken seriously Jesus's warning that the day of the Lord will come as a thief in the night, so be prepared! It was nighttime. Is this it? As a church organist, I know very well the lyrics of all those great Advent hymns that speak of the Second Coming such as, "Wake, Awake, for Night is Flying," based on Matthew 25:1–13. However, wouldn't you know it, the electricity came back on an hour later. There was no trumpet or the voice of the archangel. The sun came up, and the day went on as usual. However, that nighttime experience served as a *wake-up* call for me. It reminded me that the Word of God is truth and for real, that our time on this earth is short and fragile, as we await the fulfillment of God's kingdom.

Seminary professor, Dr. Walt Bouman reminded his students how important the *kingdom of God* is in the Christian faith. Dr. Bouman emphasized that God's kingdom certainly had arrived in the death and resurrection of Jesus, yet he added, the kingdom is both "already, but not yet." By *already*, he meant the kingdom of God is a present and eternal reality. It is not some hoped for—Shangri-la pie in the sky.

On the other hand, the kingdom is *not yet*, meaning God has not finished his plan for our salvation. He is moving forward toward a great consummation. As Christians, we live in the tension of being in both worlds at the same time—the *already* and the *not yet*. So then, what do we do? How shall we live? The exhortation from Ephesians 5:15–16 (NRSV) gives us a clue, "Be careful then, how you live, not as unwise people, but as wise, making the most of the time, because the days are evil."

Now you may be thinking, this book is supposed to be about finding humor in biblical passages, and there certainly is nothing too amusing about the passages quoted so far in this final chapter. I concur. However, I hope we can at least find joy and delight in the words, "God has destined us not for wrath but for obtaining salvation through our Lord Jesus Christ." That is such good news that it would give us good reason to laugh!

In the Introduction, I pledged not to come across as a preachy, holier-than-thou, sanctimonious, Goody Two-shoes. That has been my endeavor throughout my writing. Again, I write not as someone who has *arrived* but as a fellow traveler on the road of life. I echo these words of Paul:

> I'm not saying that I have this all together, that I have it made. But I am well on my way, reaching out for Christ, who has so wondrously reached out for me. Friends, don't get me wrong: By no means do I count myself an expert in all of this, but I've got my eye on the goal, where God is beckoning us onward—to Jesus. (Philippians 3:13–14 MSG)

A Christian writer named D. T. Niles wrote, "Evangelism is like one beggar showing another beggar where the bread is." And so, I close this *last shot* by humbly saying, I am but one beggar inviting you to where the bread is: Jesus, the bread of life.

Jesus said to them, "I am the bread of life. Whoever comes to me will never be hungry, and whoever believes in me will never be thirsty" (John 6:35 NRSV).

As a church organist, I feel I would be remiss if I didn't end with a stanza from one of the great hymns of faith, "My Hope is Built on Nothing Less" (Edward Mote, 1797–1874, alt.).

"When He shall come with trumpet sound,
Oh, may I then in Him be found,
Clothed in His righteousness alone,
Redeemed to stand before the throne!
On Christ, the solid rock, I stand;
All other ground is sinking sand."

REFERENCES

1971. *Living Bible (TLB) The Living Bible.* Carol Stream, Illinois 60188: Tyndale House Publishers Inc.

1973, 1978, 1984, 2011. *New International Version (NIV) Holy Bible, New International Version®, NIV®.* Biblica Inc.

1989. *New Revised Standard Version (NRSV) New Revised Standard Version Bible.* Division of Christian Education of the National Council of the Churches of Christ in the United States of America.

1992. *Good News Translation (GNT).* The American Bible Society.

1995, 2003, 2013, 2014, 2019, 2020. *God's Word Translation (GW).* God's Word to the Nations Mission Society.

1996, 2004, 2015. *New Living Translation (NLT) Holy Bible, New Living Translation.* Carol Stream, Illinois 60188: Tyndale House Publishers, Inc.

Peterson, Eugene. 1993, 2002, 2018. *The Message (MSG).*

2016. *English Standard Version (ESV) The Holy Bible, English Standard Version. ESV® Text Edition.* Crossway Bibles, a publishing ministry of Good News Publishers.

Schuller, Robert H. 1998. *Success is Never Ending, Failure Is Never Final.* Nashville: Thomas Nelson Publishers.

Sell, Charles M. 1989. *Unfinished Business.* Portland, OR: Multnomah Books.

About the Author

Dale T. Stanton has been a lifelong church musician since his early teen years. Dale holds a bachelor of music (BMus) degree from Wayne State University, Detroit, Michigan, a master of divinity (MDiv) degree from Trinity Lutheran Seminary, Columbus, Ohio, and a master of science (MS) degree in counseling psychology from Troy State University, Dothan, Alabama. Dale also possesses a private pilot certificate. In addition, he holds a diploma in piano tuning and repair and freelances as a piano technician. Dale is an ordained pastor and served several congregations of the former American Lutheran Church. He also worked as a trained counselor and social worker. Dale is a professional church organist, hymn writer, and a composer of musical voluntaries for the church service. In addition to playing the organ, he enjoys time at the piano, the hammer dulcimer, and finds pleasure in gardening and helping his wife, Beth, with the care of the family pet cats. Dale and Beth have one adult son, Benjamin, who conceived the title for this book.

CPSIA information can be obtained
at www.ICGtesting.com
Printed in the USA
BVHW071406210222
629667BV00002B/197